HOW TO DRAW CHIBI
A step by step guide in learning to draw Chibi

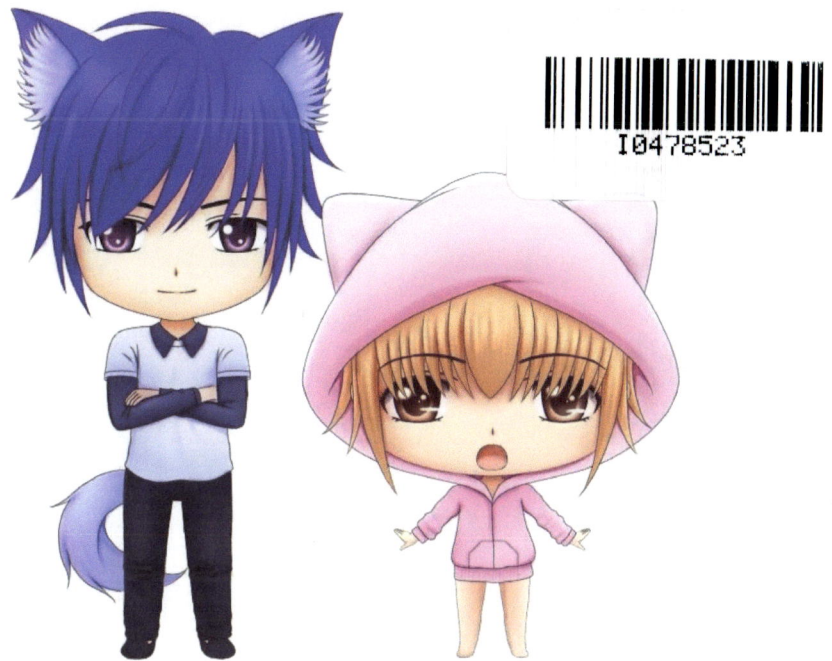

I0478523

Learn to Draw Series

William T. Dela Peña Jr.

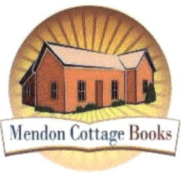

Mendon Cottage Books

JD-Biz Publishing

Learn How to Draw Books for the Absolute Beginner

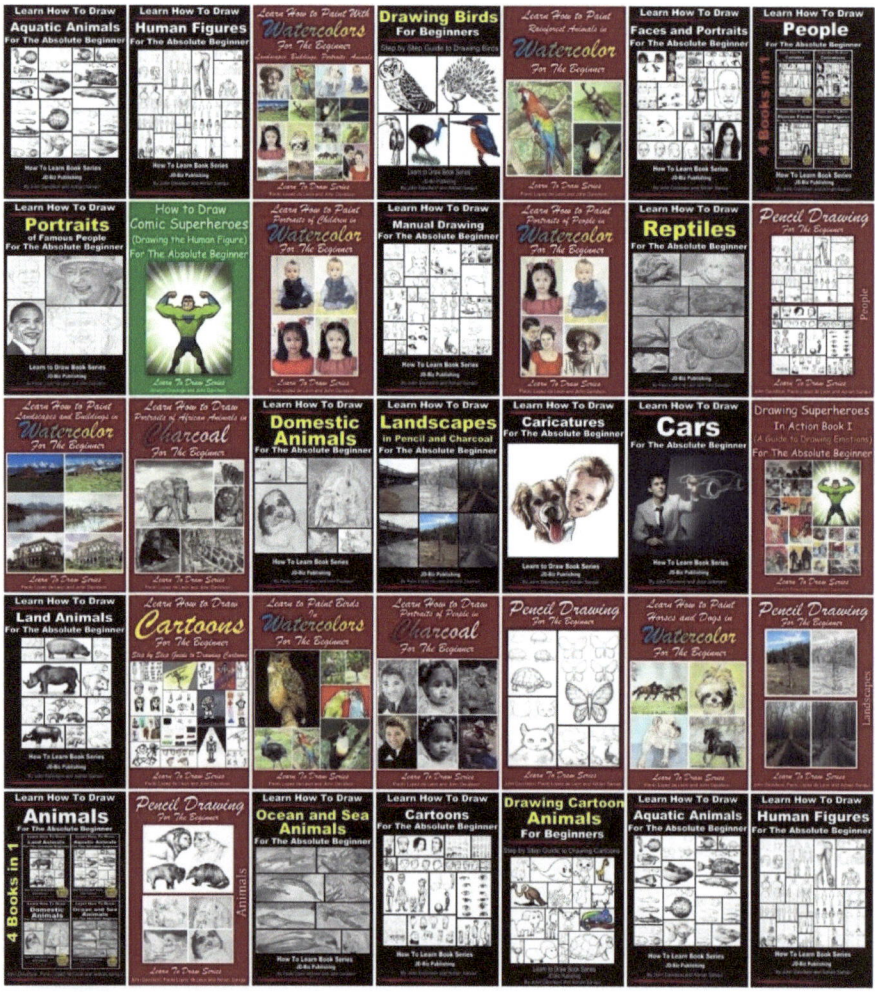

Table of Contents

INTRODUCTION

"Chibi" is a term in Japanese that describe small things and used in anime/manga to describe a character that is drawn in a short and deformed version. This art style originated in Japan, and it became popular because of its appeal and cuteness. Drawing chibi can be fun and enjoyable. In this book, you will learn how to draw step by step, chibis in an easy and effective way that is very helpful to beginners.

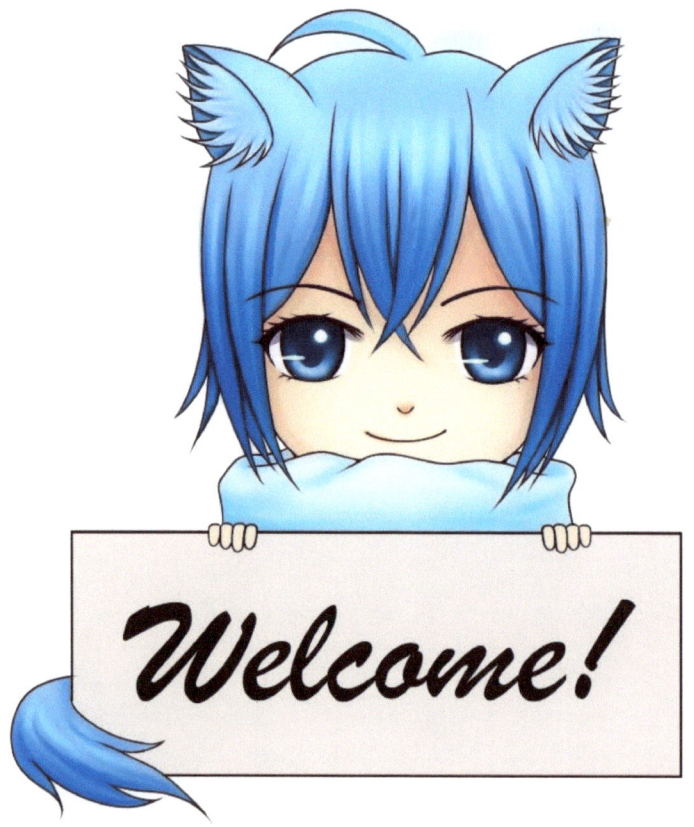

HOW TO DRAW CHIBI

Drawing chibi is somewhat difficult for a beginner at first, so before you draw you must have a basic idea on how to do it so that, it doesn't look weird.

First, you must know the body proportion. A chibi usually stands approximately two heads tall and the head is larger than its body, this is the common proportion of chibi.

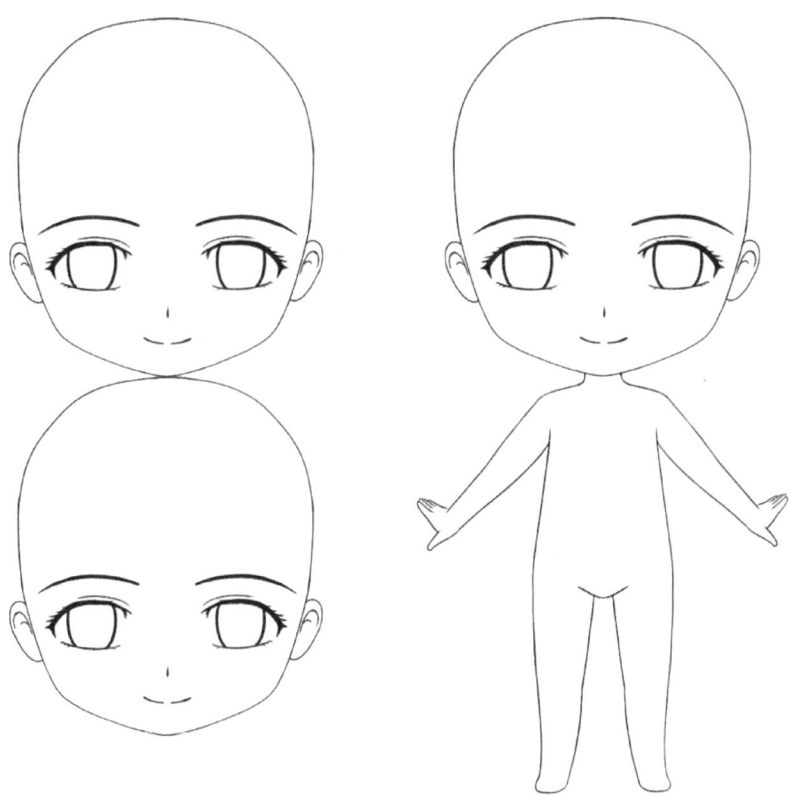

DRAWING THE HEAD

First, draw a circle, it does not need to be a perfect circle just draw it roughly and after that draw a vertical line at the center of the circle.

Step: 1   Step: 2

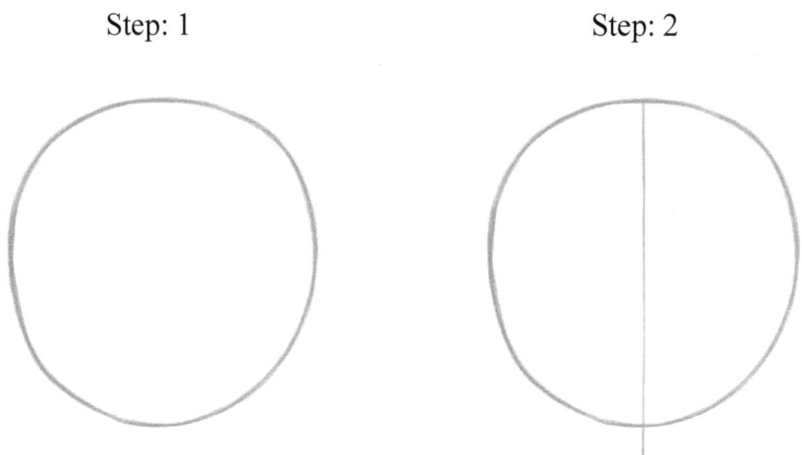

Then draw a horizontal line below the center of the circle as shown in the picture below and after that draw, another horizontal line and this will be the guideline for drawing the eyes.

Step: 3   Step: 4

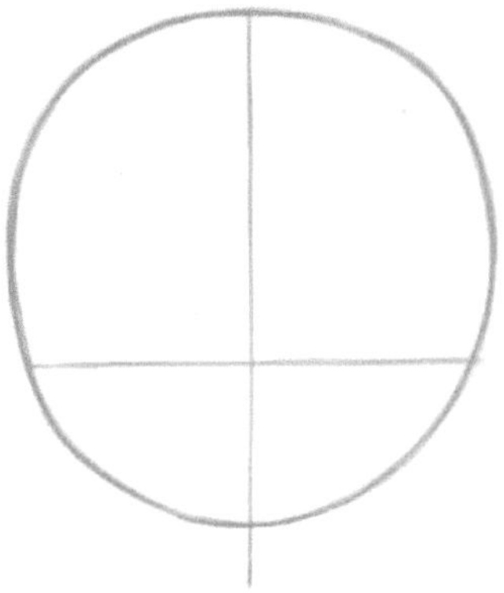

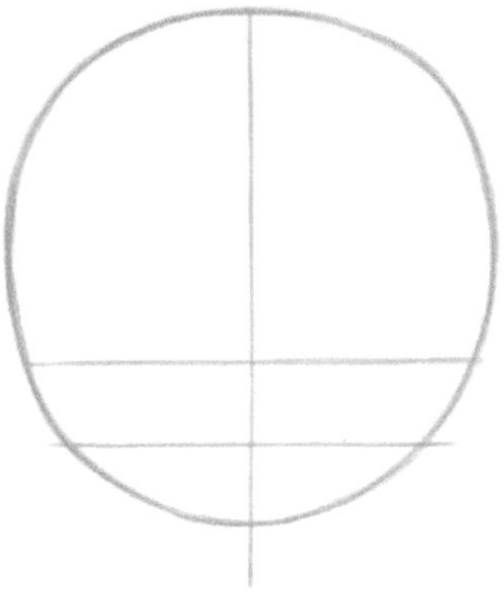

Then draw again a horizontal line below the outside of the circle this will be the guide for drawing the jaw line.

Step: 5

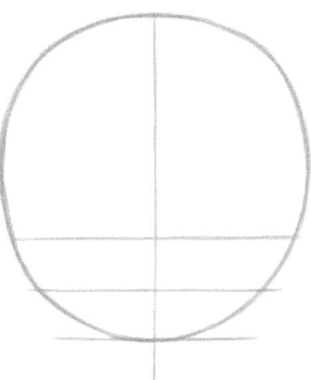

Then draw a line that connects to the upper horizontal line and to the vertical line; then do it on the opposite side as shown in the picture below.

Step: 6

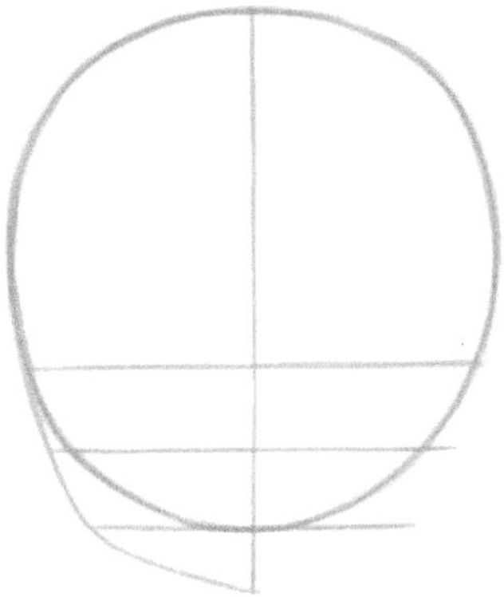

Step: 7

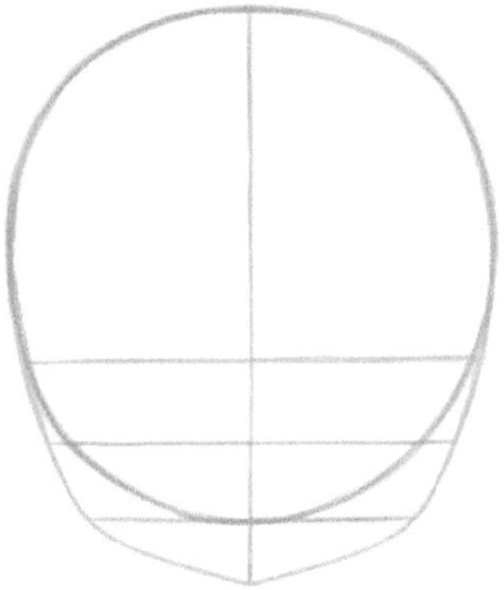

Step: 8

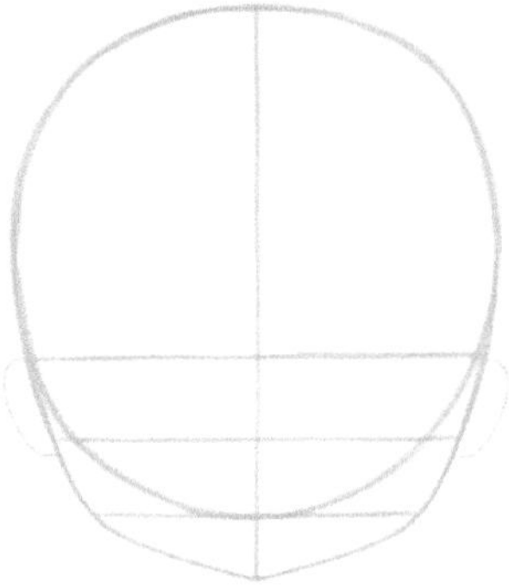

DRAWING THE BODY

The guidelines in making the head of the chibi are already finished, now it's time to draw the guidelines for the body.

In drawing the body, imagine the shape of an ice cream stick it is thinner at the top and fuller at the bottom.

Step: 9

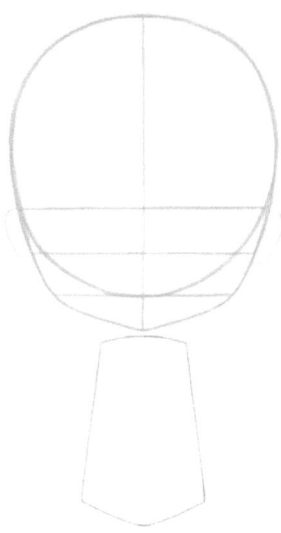

Then lastly, draw the arms, the hands, and the legs. Keep in mind, that when drawing the legs keep it a flowing line, not just in a regular cylinder shape. Also, think about the masses of the legs.

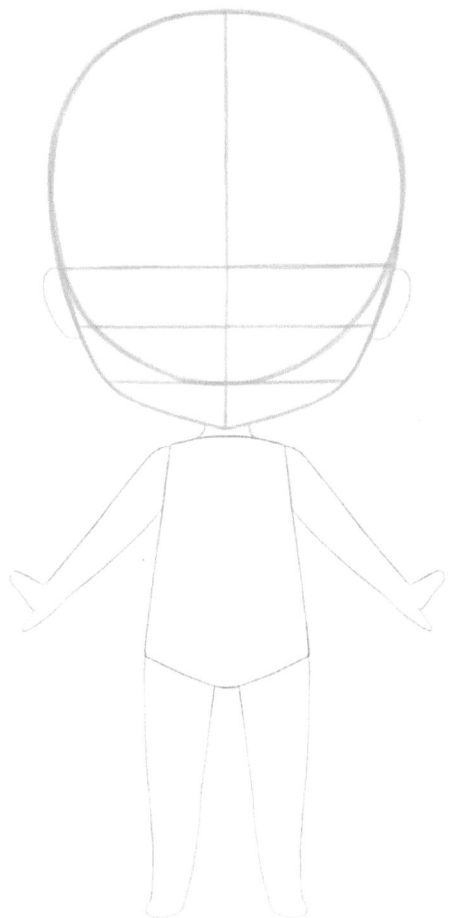

OUTLINING

Start outlining the head first, before going to the other parts so that it will have a consistent flow of work. Detail from the top going down. And keep in mind not to draw dark and thick lines so that you can still erase it if you commit a mistake.

Then draw the facial features. Use the guidelines to locate the landmarks of each feature, as shown in the picture below. When drawing a female face make the mouth expressive and add eyelashes.

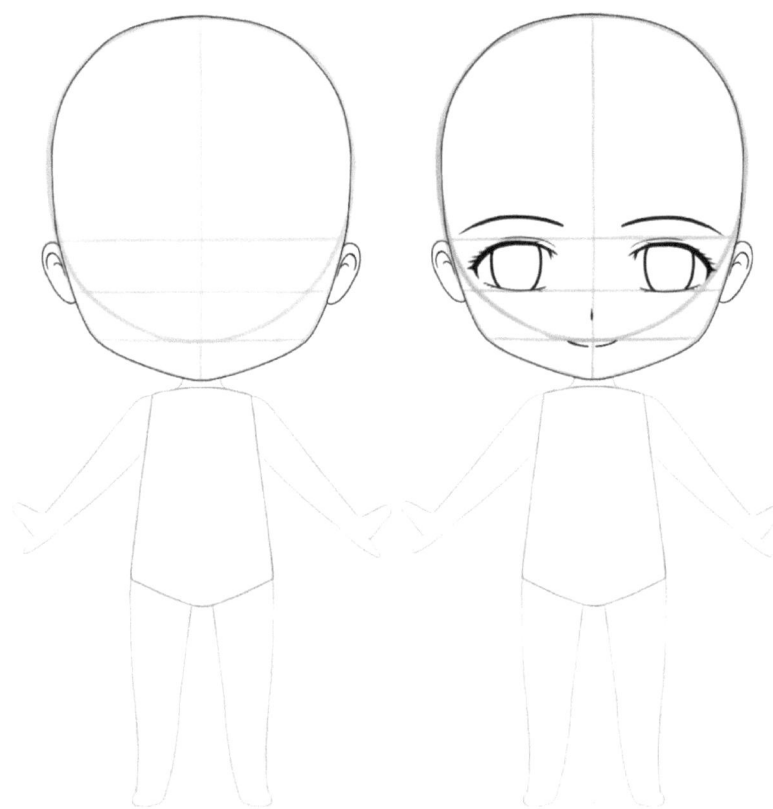

Then remove the guidelines because we don't need them anymore and remove all the unnecessary lines and make a clean version of it like the picture below on the left, and now our chibi base is ready for now.

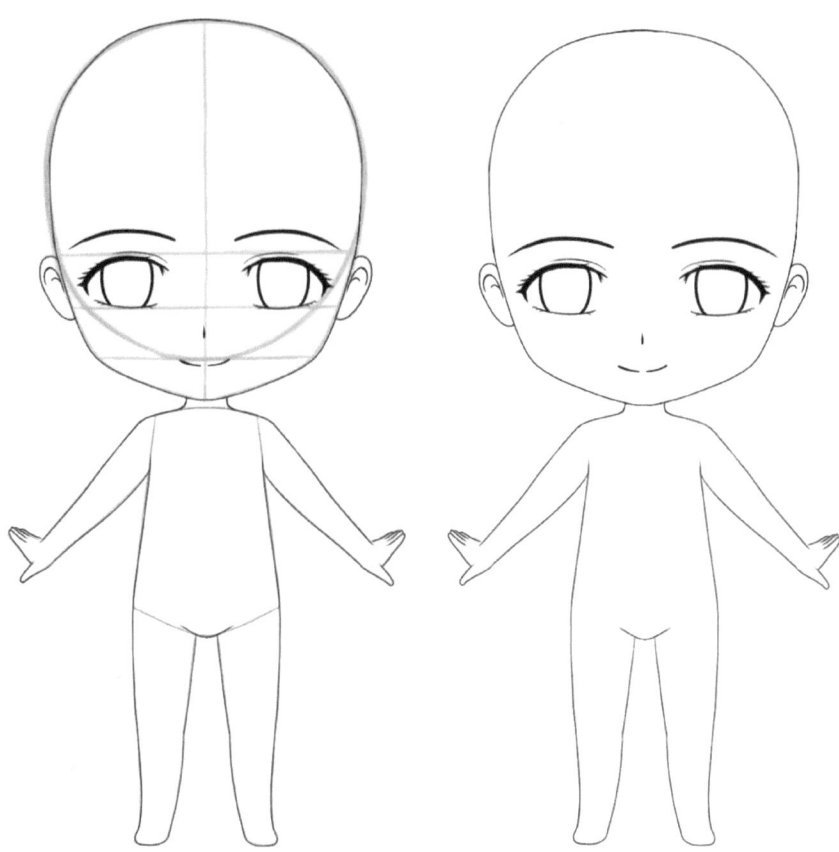

Next we will be adding hair and clothes to the base. Think of a cute and fluffy hair style. And just make the clothes simple. In my case, I make the base of my chibi a school girl.

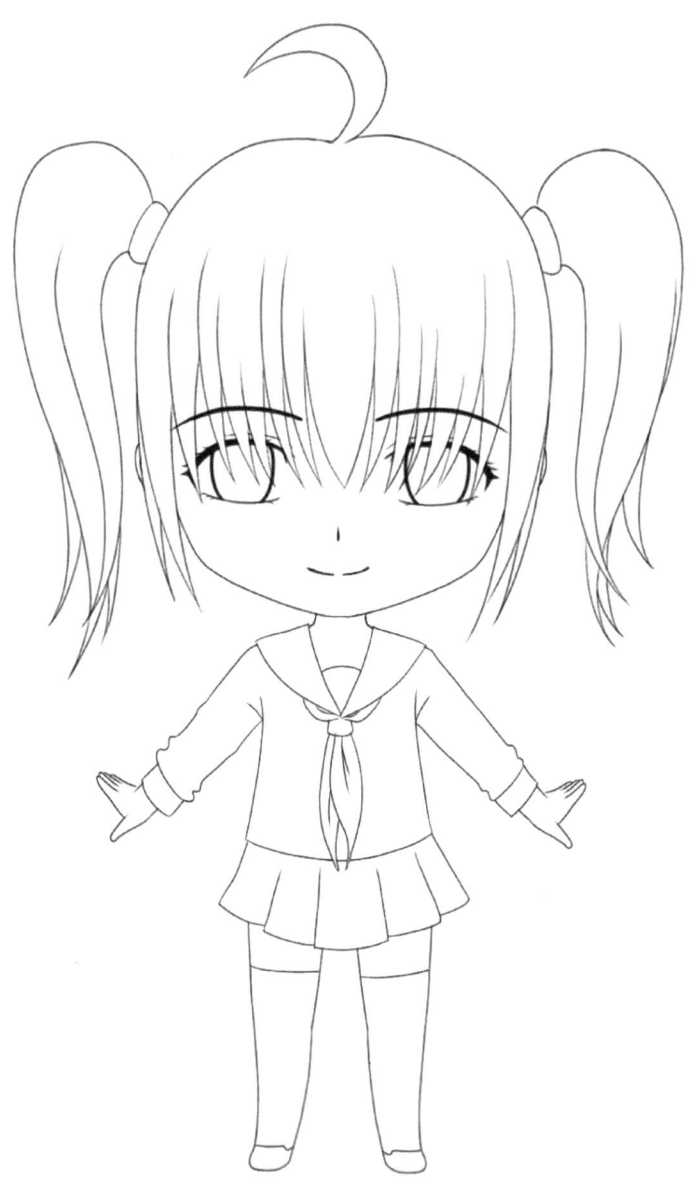

COLORING A CHIBI

This is the colored version, in coloring chibi put some extra highlight in the eyes to make it more appealing and innocent looking, avoid overdoing it on the shading, just make the shading simple.

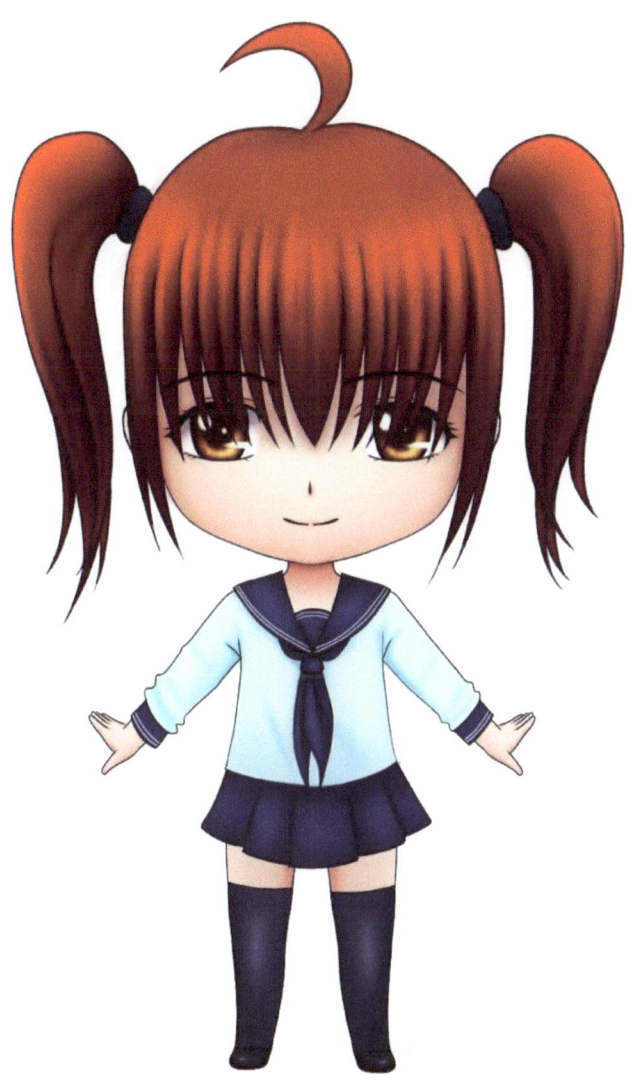

So now you've learned how to make a chibi base for a girl, now I'm going to show you how to draw chibi base for a boy like in the picture below, drawing it is pretty similar to drawing the chibi base of a girl.

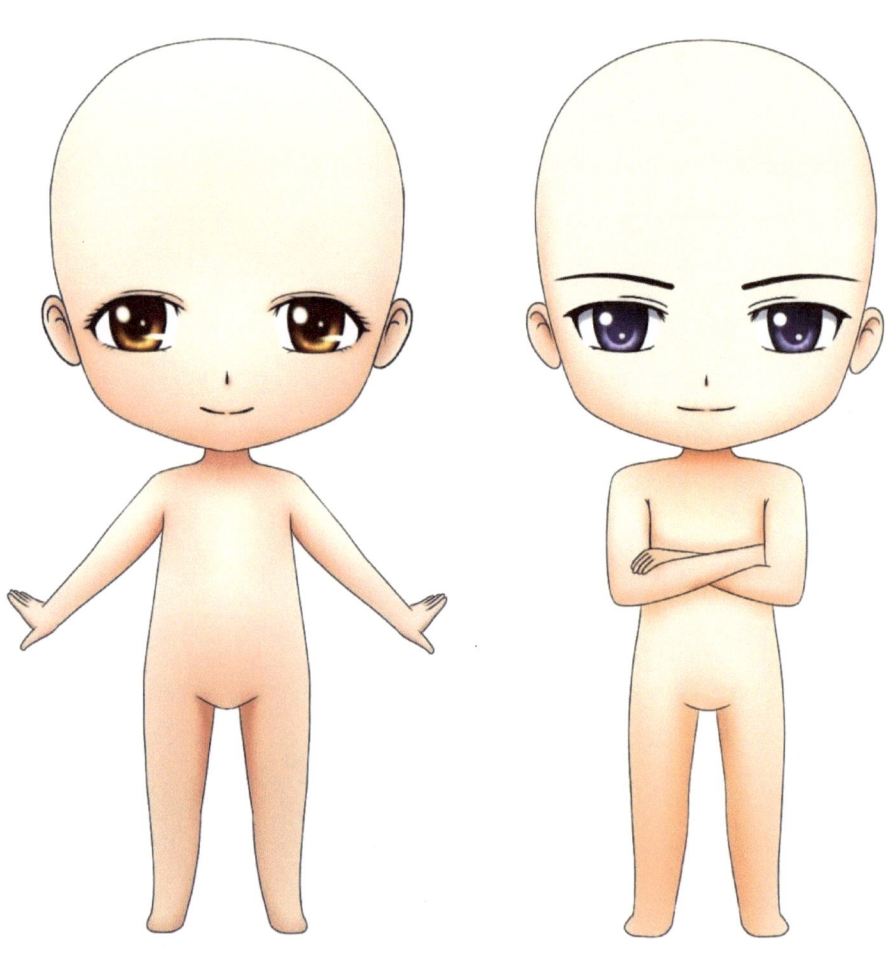

DRAWING A MALE CHIBI

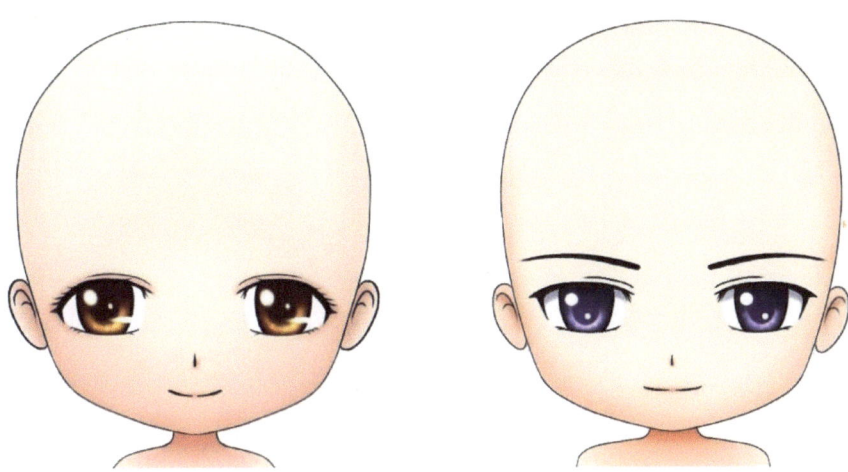

Observe the difference of the shape of the head. Male chibi has a lower jaw line so keep in mind this key point in drawing a male chibi.

This is just optional, this time, try to refrain from using guidelines. Don't become a slave to using guidelines because it will make you draw slower. First, draw the head and draw a cross as a guideline to the facial features, this is what I do but if you can't do it you can use the guidelines.

Step: 1   Step: 2

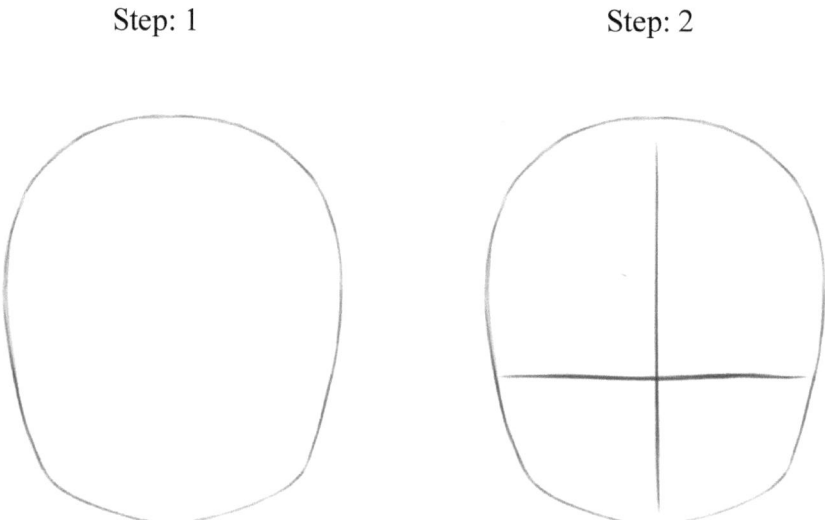

DRAWING THE MALE CHIBI BODY

Drawing the male body is just like drawing the female body go back to the previous page to recall it. To make it more masculine think of a pose that is suitable for a male.

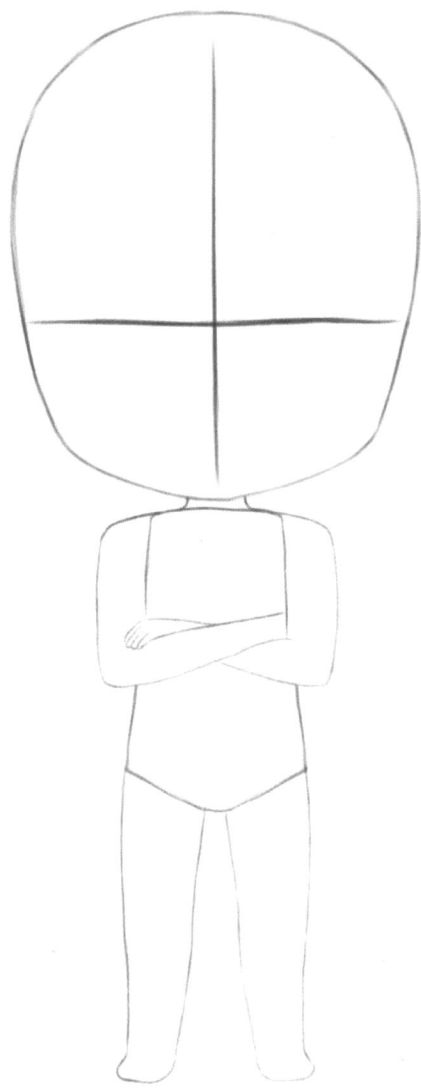

Draw the eyes below the cross line as shown in the picture below. Keep in mind when drawing the male eyes make them sharp and don't put eyelashes, make the smile less expressive and just draw a dot to represent the nose.

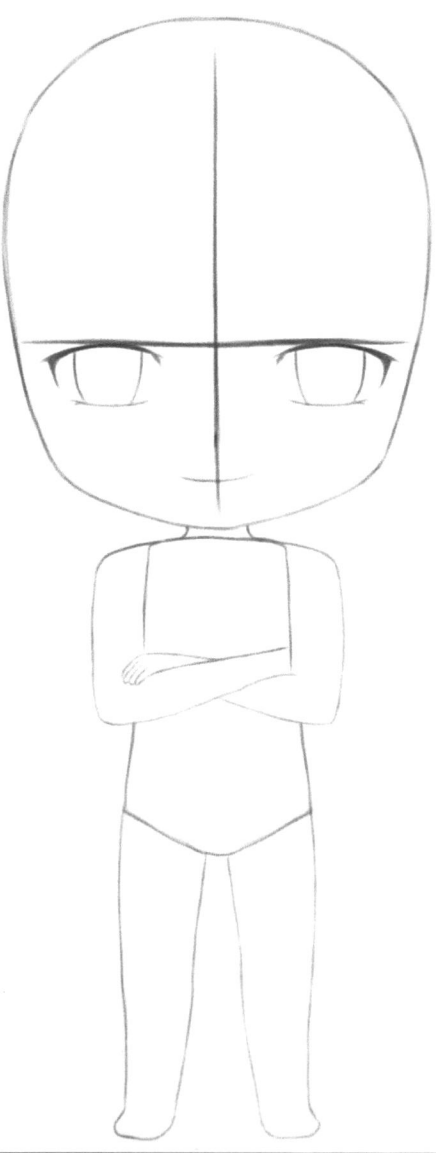

Then draw the eyebrows. Make sure to keep in mind the eyebrows need to be thick and sharp looking and make the position lower inside, as shown in the picture below then draw a crease at the top of the eyes and draw the ears.

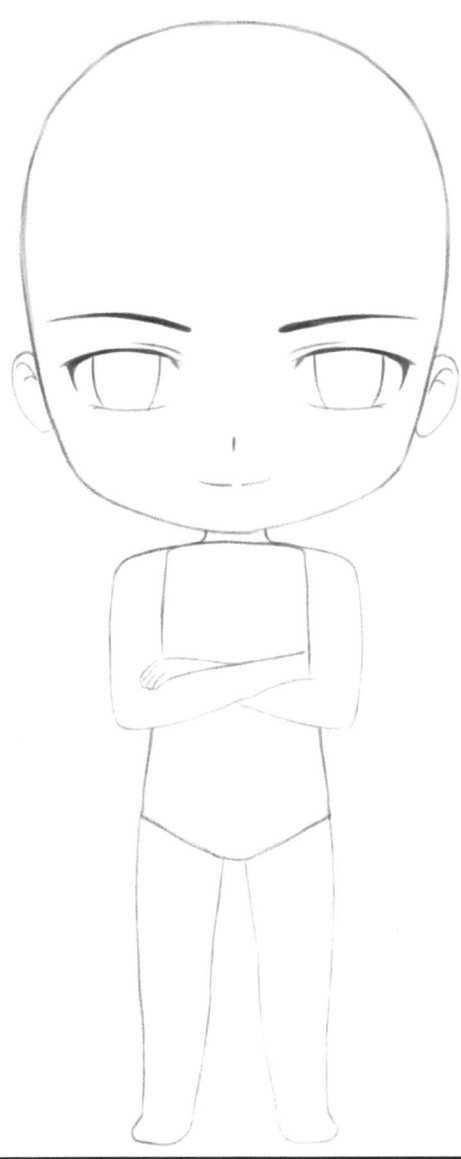

Then outline it with a black ink. To make it precise, draw just one stroke with accuracy and confidence, because theslower you apply the ink the more imperfections will come out. Just be patience, inking takes time to get it right.

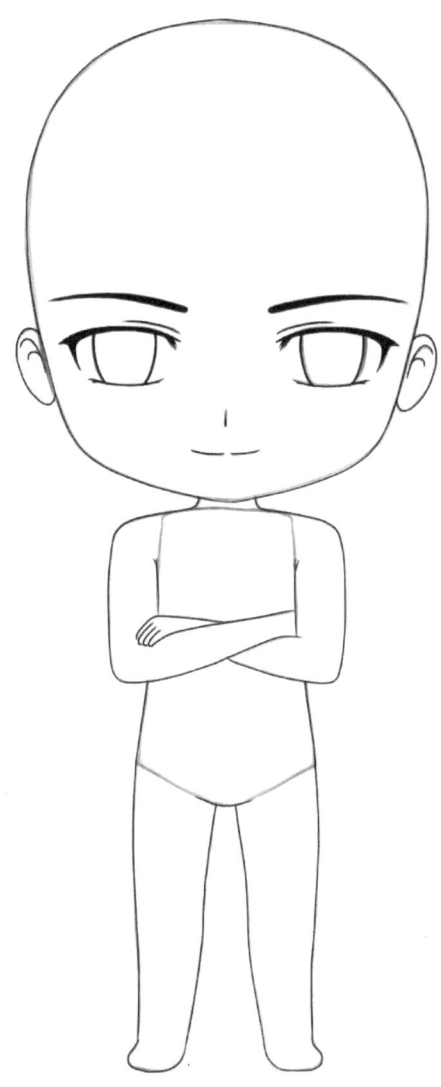

Then remove the guidelines and extra lines like the picture below then keep it, for your template when drawing a male chibi. You can scan it and edit on a photo editing software or trace it.

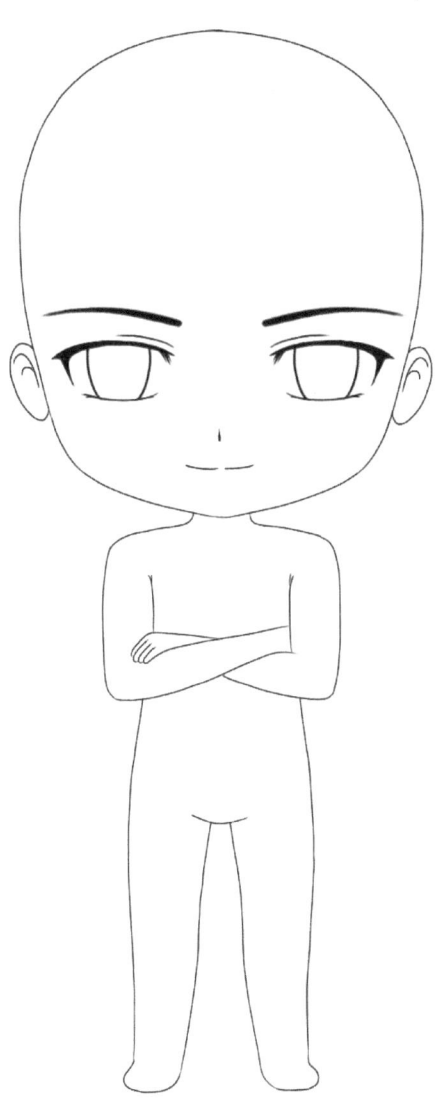

HOW TO DRAW A CAT EARS

Now I going to teach you how to draw cat ears that I will use as an accessory to the chibi male that I created. First, draw the base and keep in mind to draw flowing lines outside the ears.

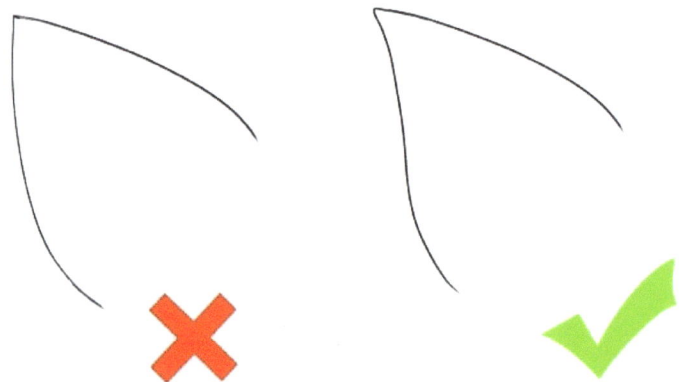

Then draw a curve line that divides the ear into sections, this will give the ear depth and it looks almost done already.

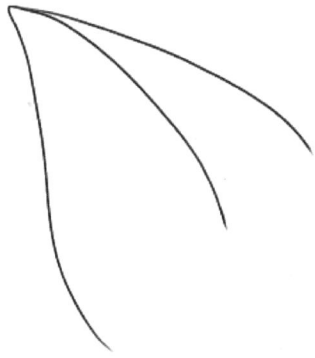

Lastly, put some fur inside the ear. The red dashed line represents the boundary of the fur so basically some of the fur goes outside below the lower portion of the ear.

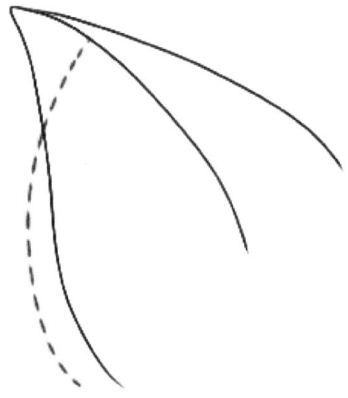

Then draw the fur, keep in mind to draw it randomized to make it natural looking then erase the overlapping portions.

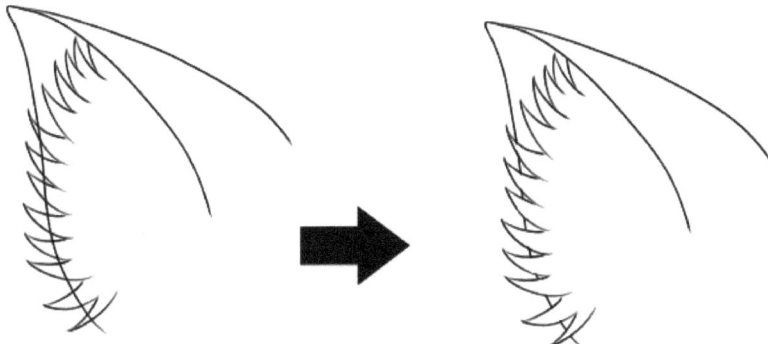

PLACING THE CAT EARS

The picture below looks nice with cat ears but the placement of the ears is off the hair should not overlap the ears.

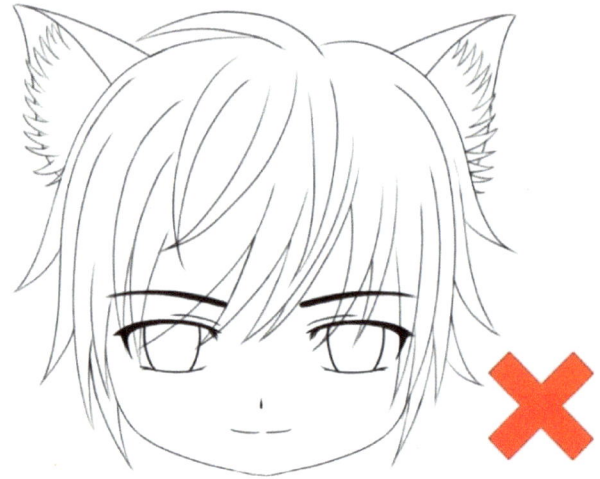

Instead, the ears should overlap the hair.

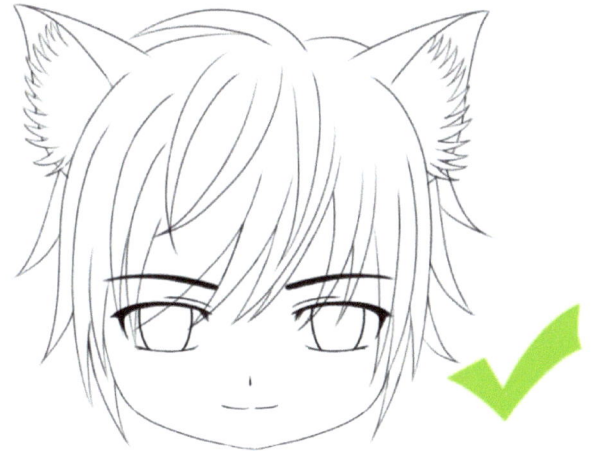

So this is now the male chibi base after adding some clothing and cat ears, I also add a tail to make it look cute.

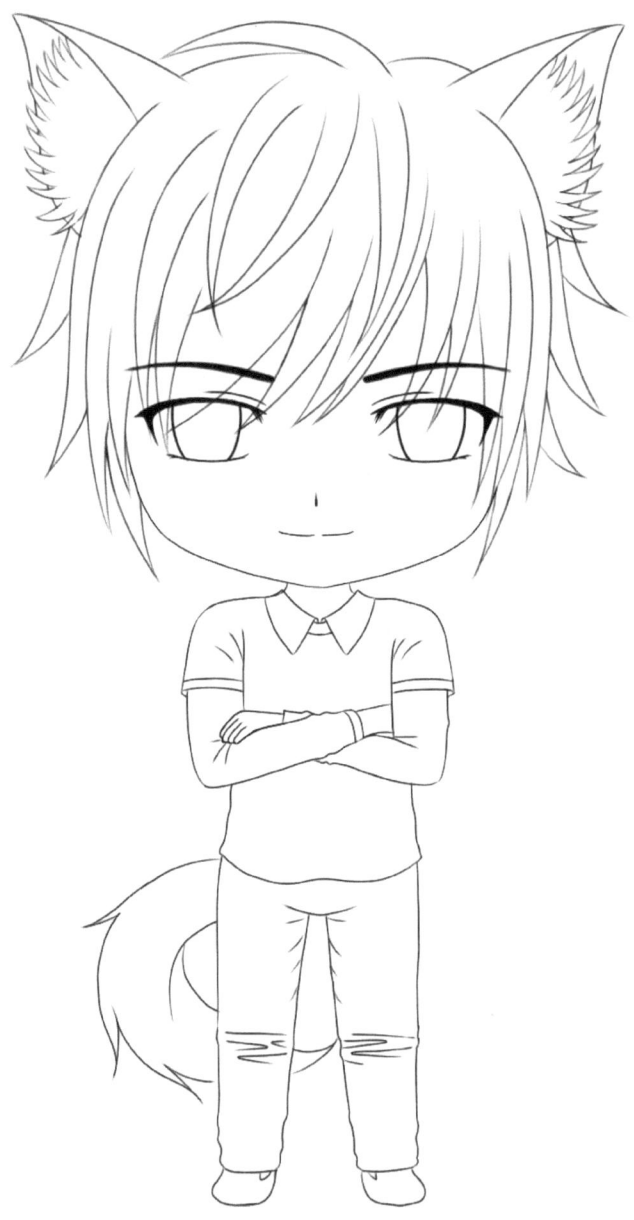

This is now the colored version. When choosing colors I recommend to use relative colors don't mix warm colors with cold colors and use colors that are in the same range of hues.

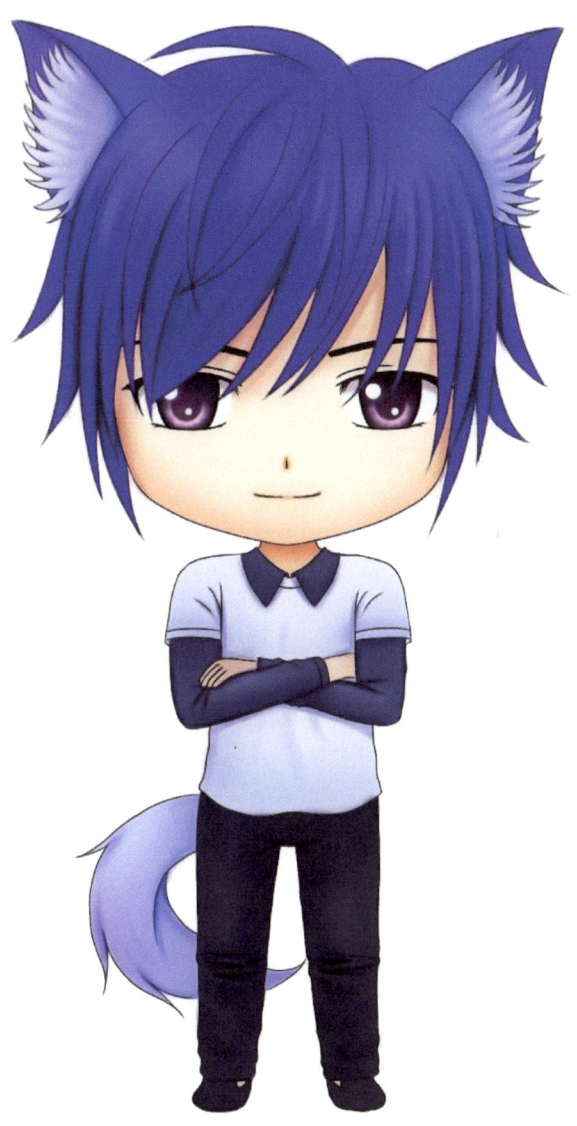

DRAWING A STYLIZED CHIBI

Next, I'm going to teach you how I stylize a chibi don't just focus on one regular way to draw chibi try to experiment and create a unique style of a chibi.

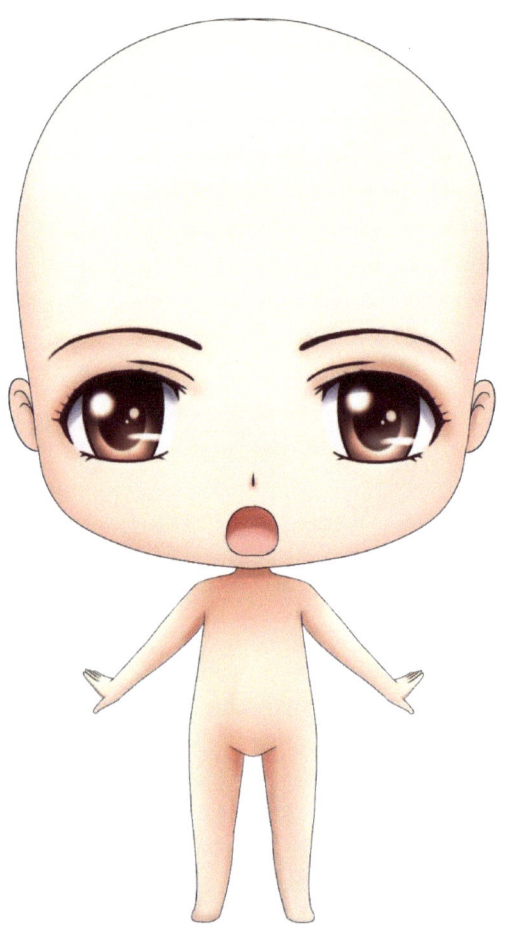

What I did is I exaggerate the shape of the head and make it wider than usual and I also exaggerate the chicks to make it look cuter.

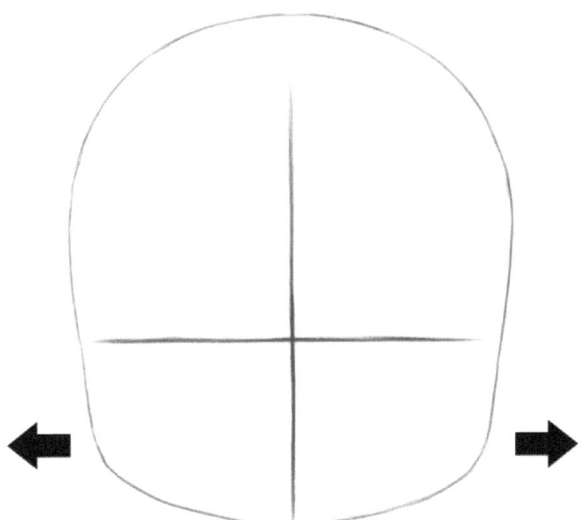

Then I also makebigger and fuller eyes than usual and drew a mouth that would fit the expressions of the eyes.

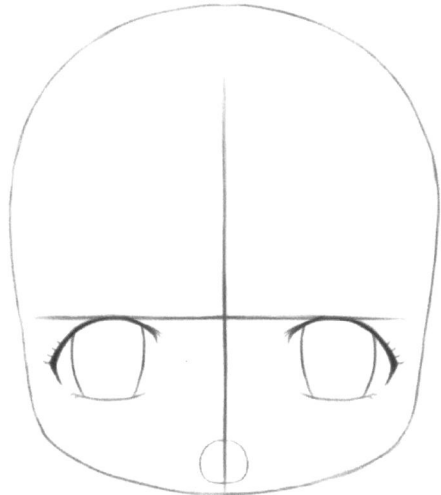

Another modification I made was to the height, I made is shorter than usual. When establishing the height keep in mind it is just approximately two heads tall or shorter than that.

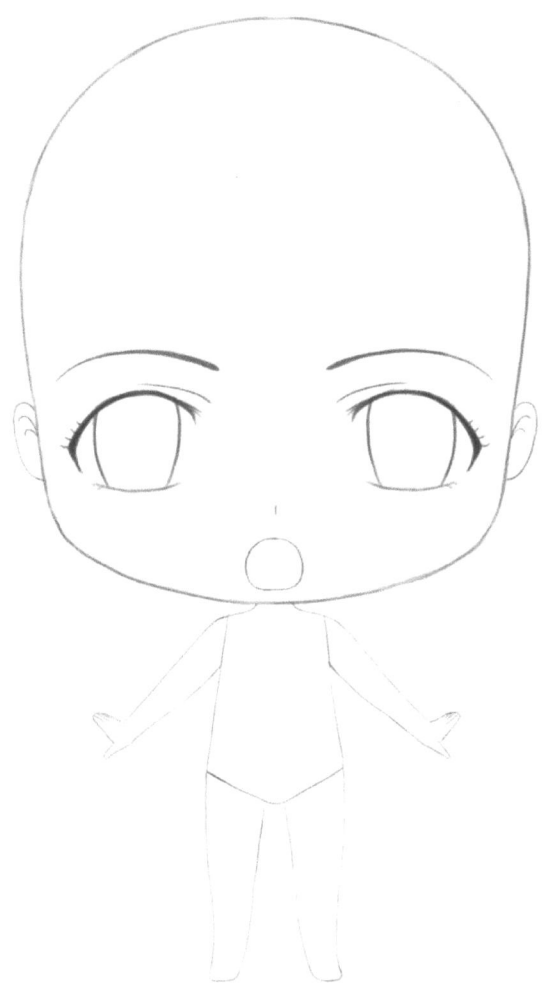

HOW TO DRAW A HOOD

In this next tutorial, I'm going to teach you how to draw a hood, this I will use to stylized my chibi.

First, draw a line that enclosed the whole head and the neck. Take note the shape of the path as shown in the picture below.

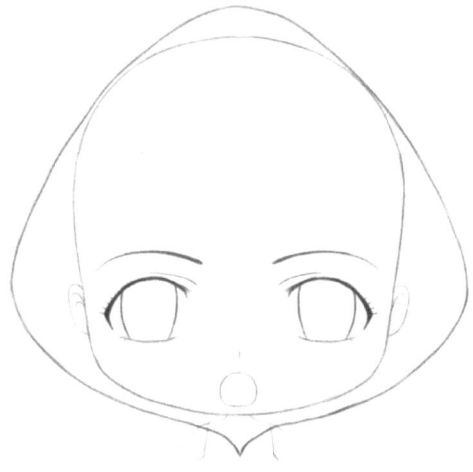

Then draw a line in the middle of the head as shown in the picture.

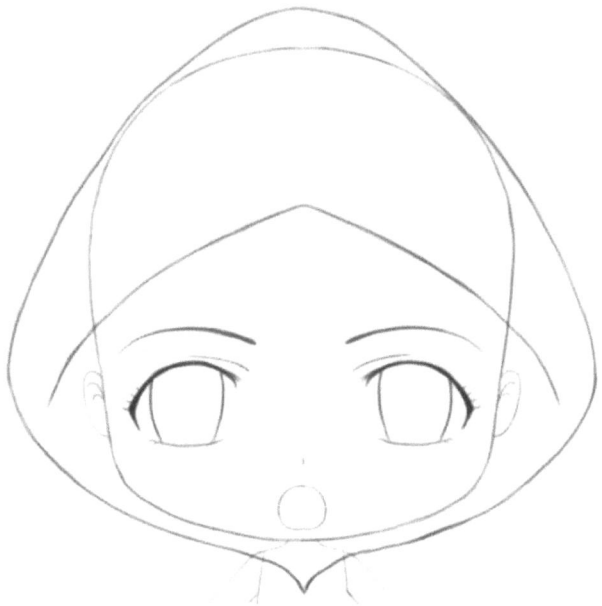

Erase some of the lines on the head that overlap the hood.

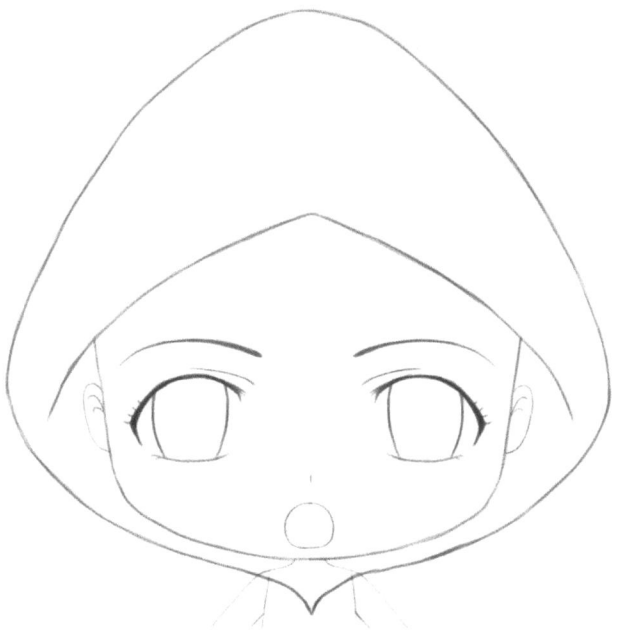

Then draw the hair and after that erase the lines that overlap the hair.

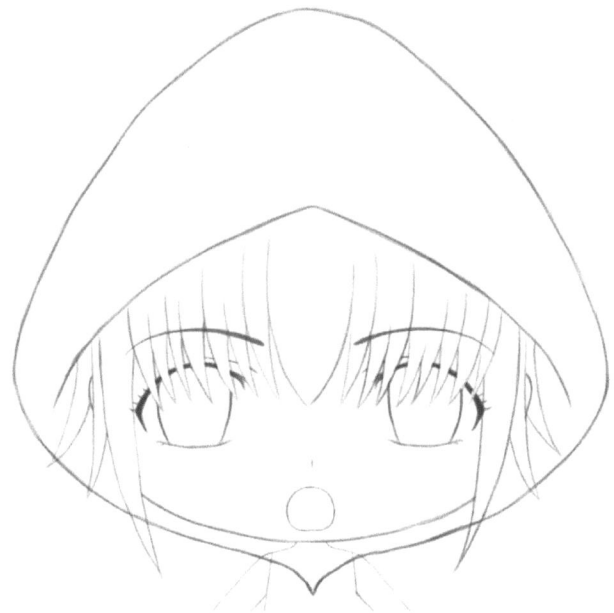

Then lastly Ifinish drawing all the clothes, I also add ears to the hood to make it look, again, cuter.

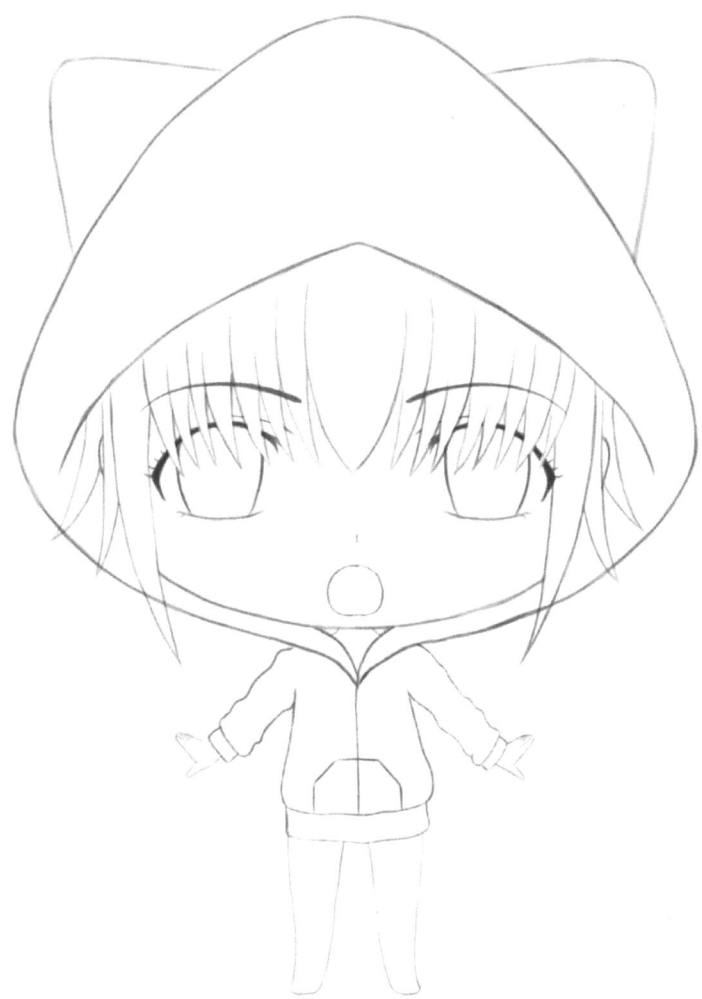

This the colored and final version.

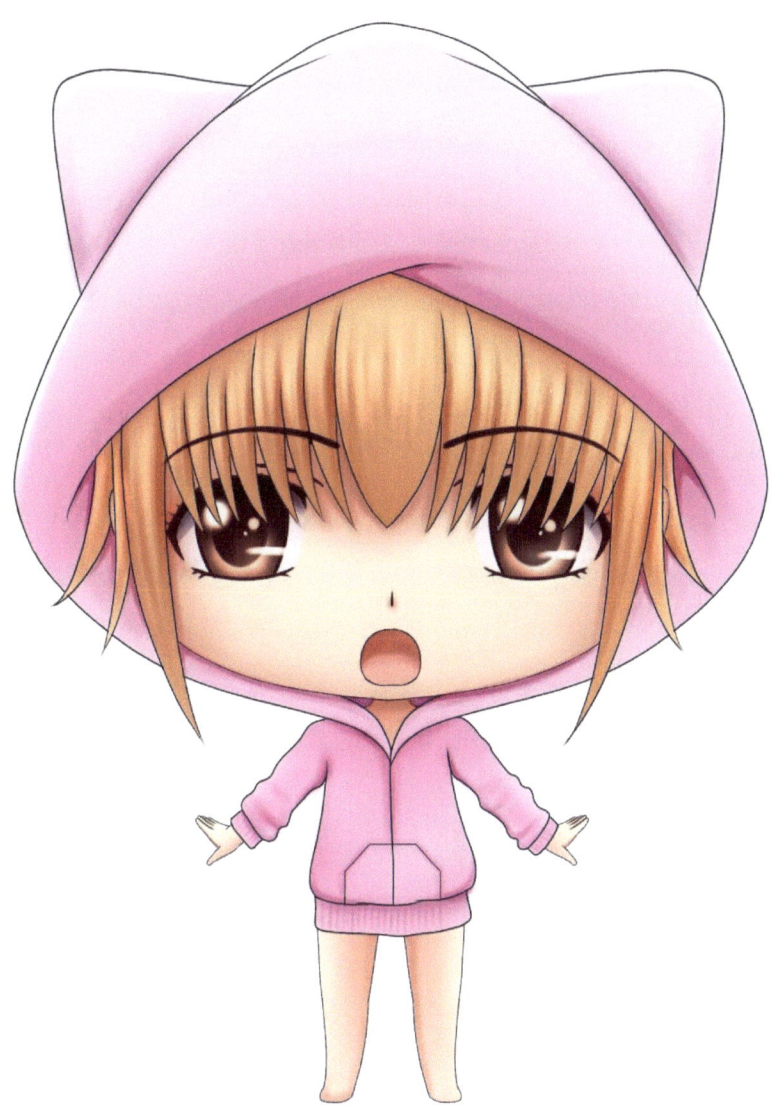

I hope you have learned a lot in my tutorial on how to draw a chibi.

Author Bio

William T. Dela Peña Jr.

William T. Dela Pena Jr. was born in Tondo, Manila but he grew up in their province in Delfin Albano, Isabela. When he was a child his parents and his relatives always get mad at him, because of his unusual behaviour, he is hyperactive and filled with curiosity around his surroundings. He always draws what he see and what he think and from there he discovered his passion for arts. During his school years, he earned a lot of awards in art competitions.

He took BS in Information Technology, but unfortunately, he was not able to finish his course due to some reasons. Then he decided to go back to Manila and to work as a graphic artist. While he was working as a graphic artist, he spends his free time in drawing anime then his friends that are Otakus notice that he has a potential in drawing manga then his friend encourages him to get involved in manga industry and he started working as a freelance manga illustrator.

Check out some of the other JD-Biz Publishing books

Gardening Series on Amazon

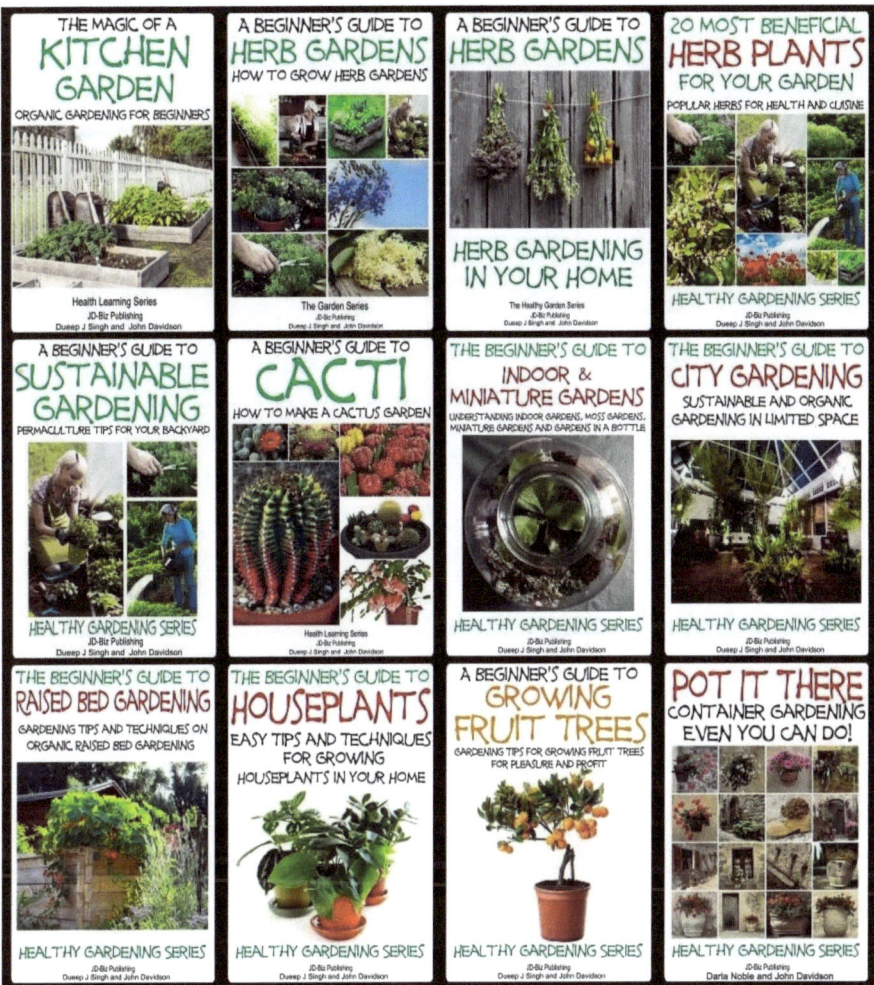

Download Free Books!

http://MendonCottageBooks.com

Health Learning Series

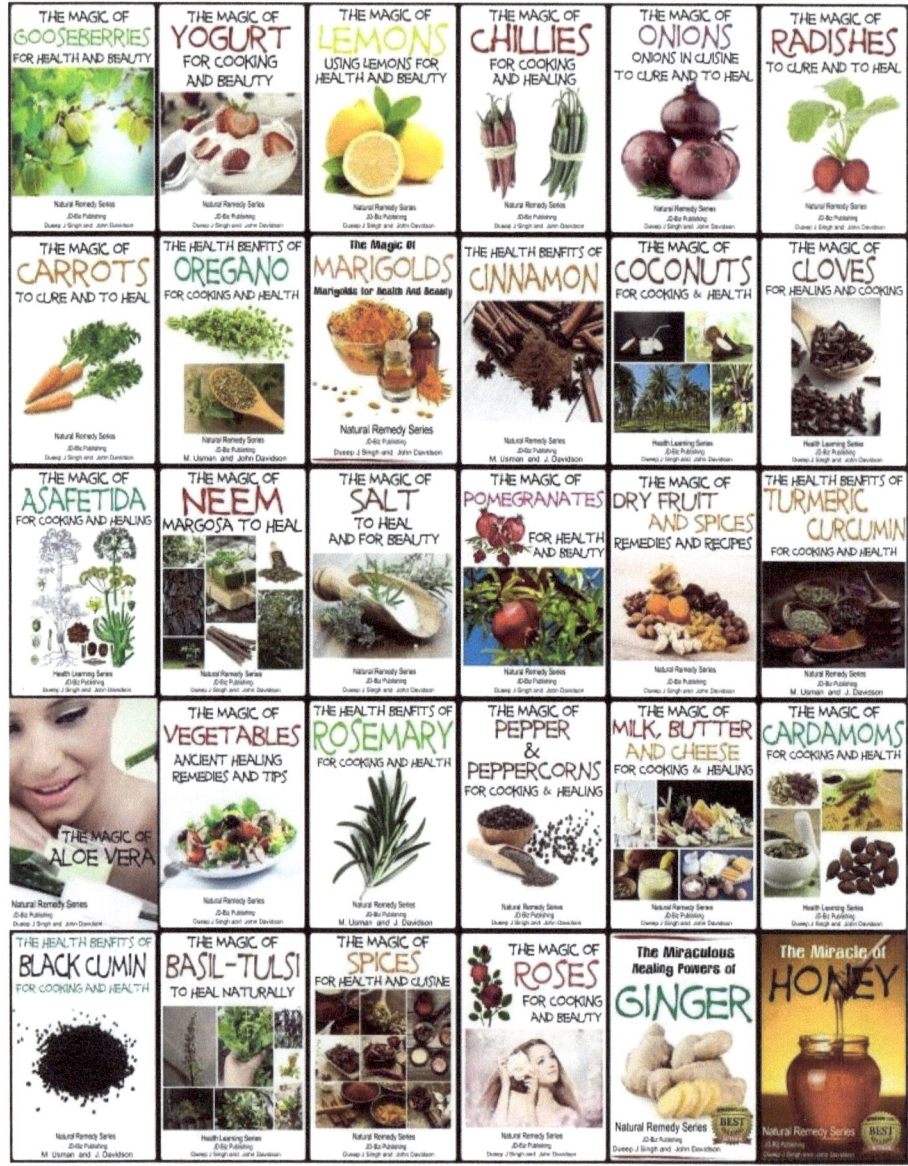

Country Life Books

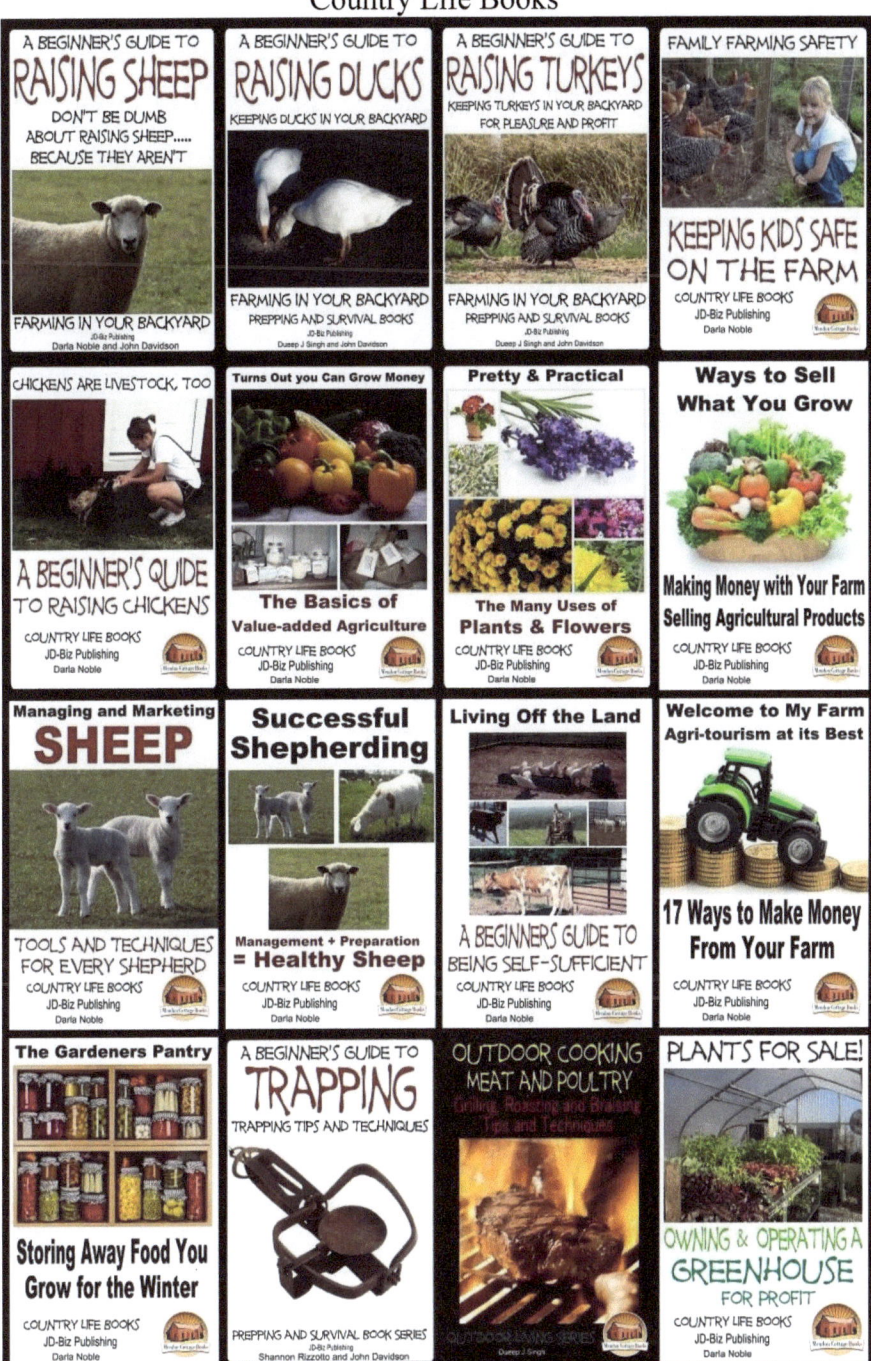

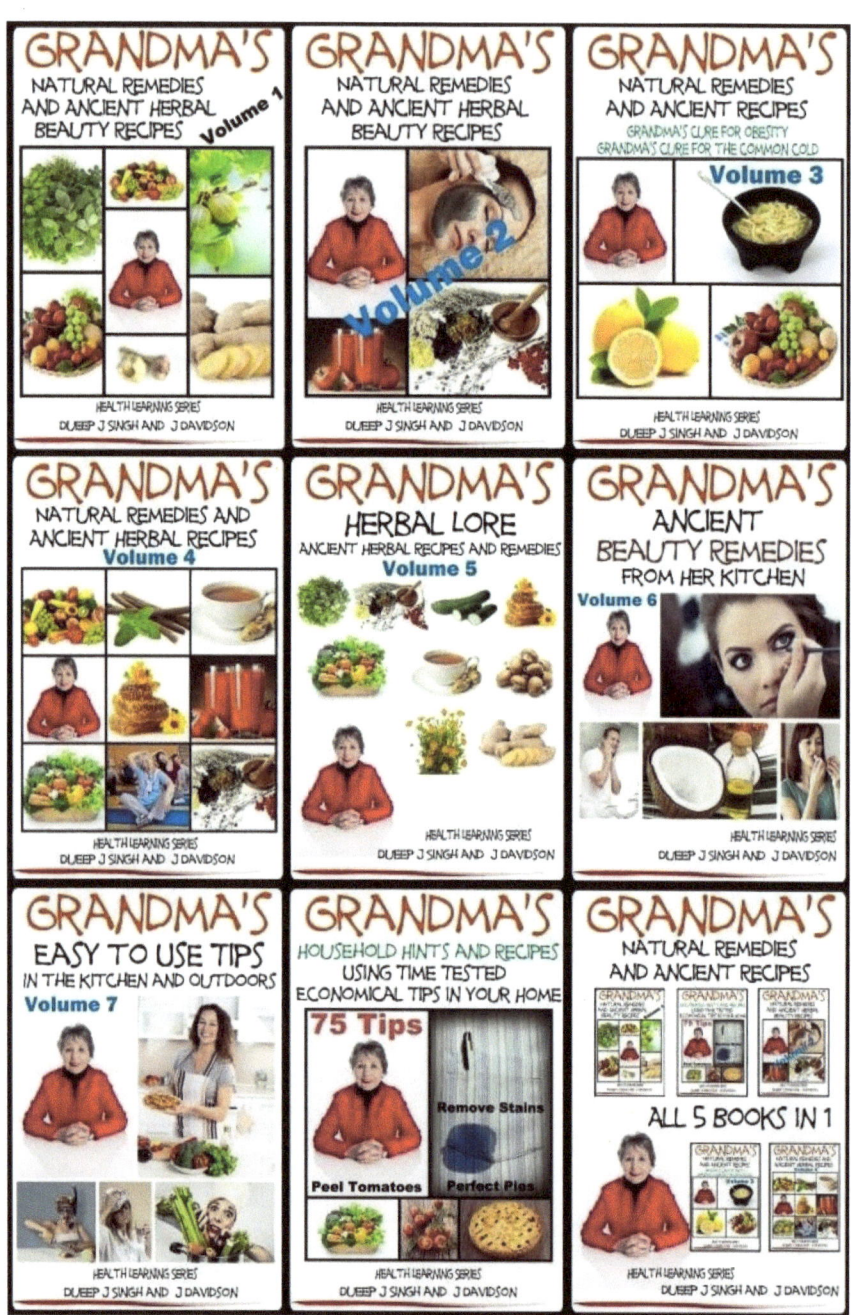

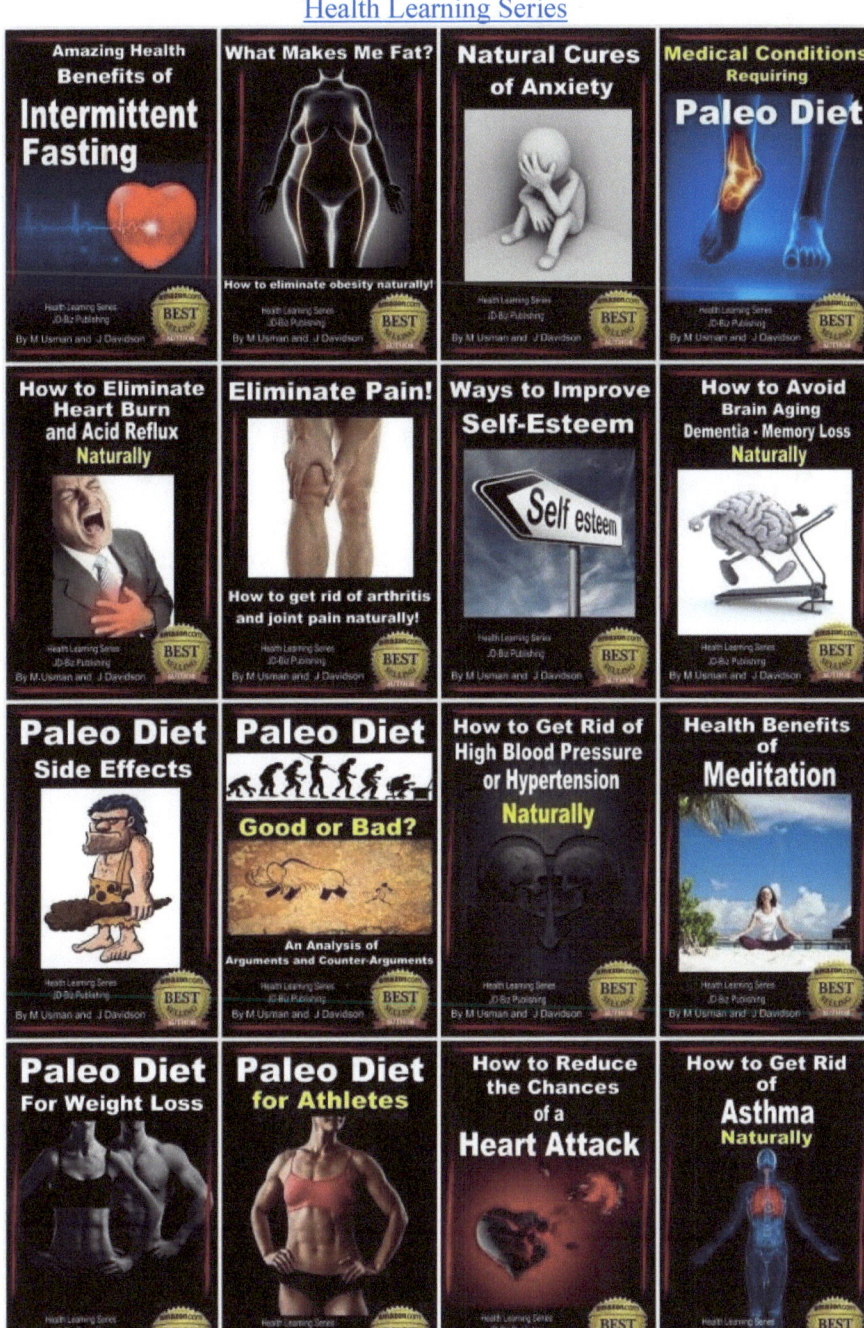

Amazing Animal Book Series

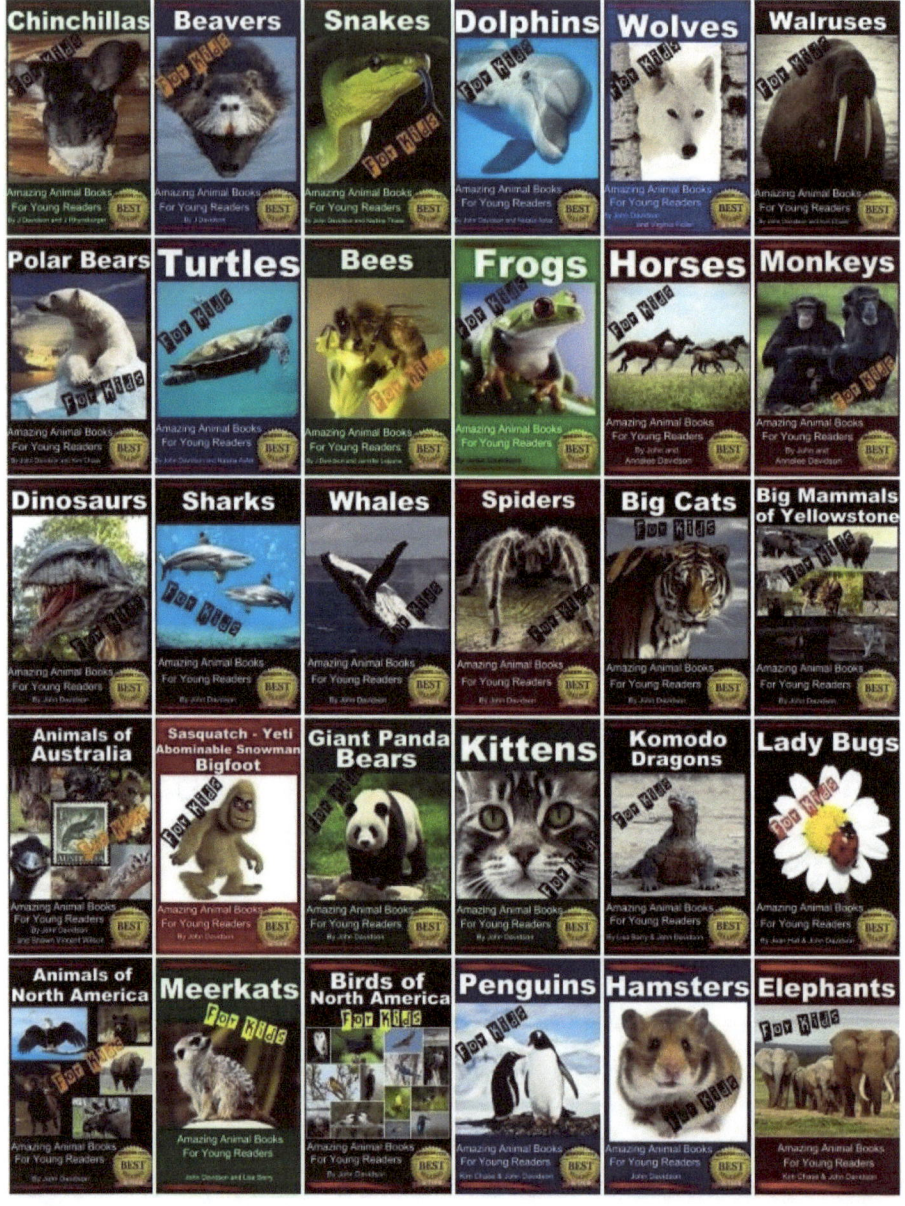

Learn To Draw Series

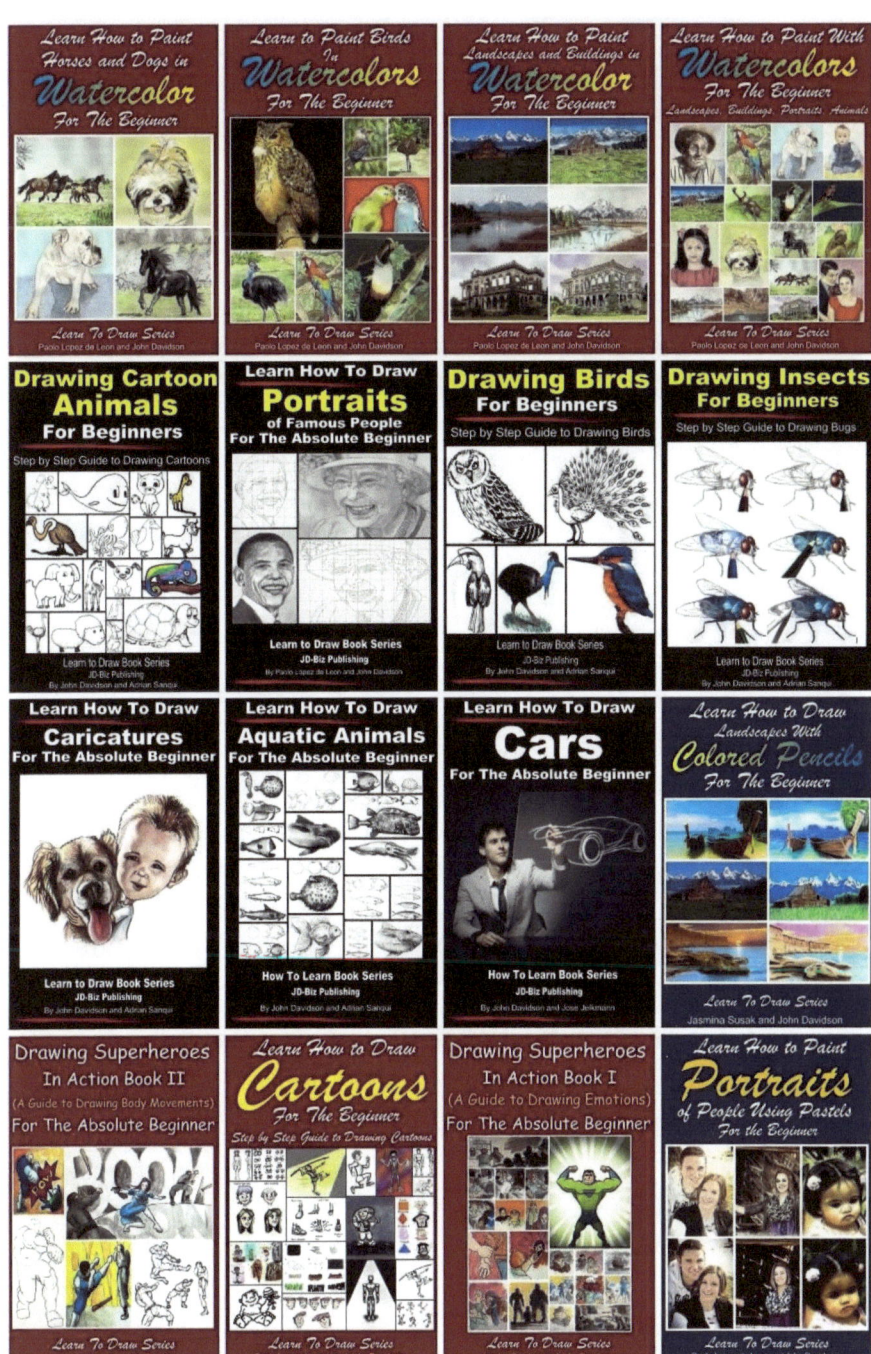

How to Build and Plan Books

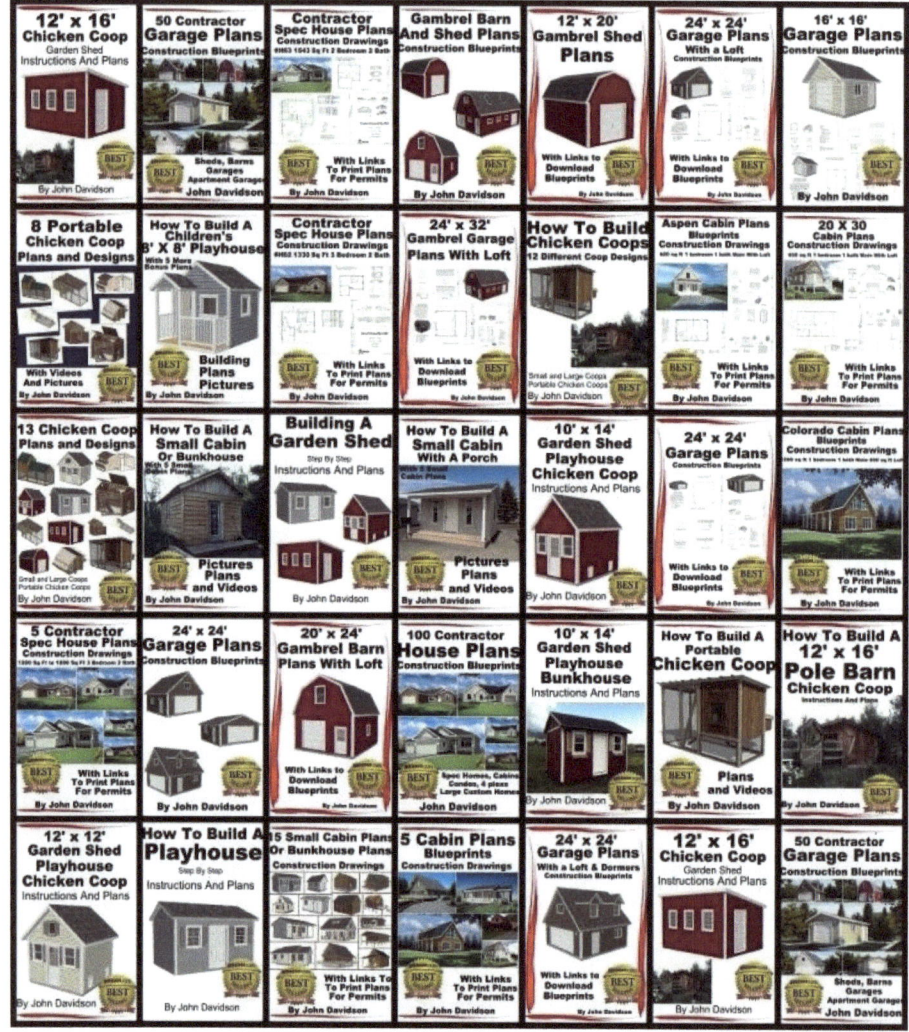

Entrepreneur Book Series

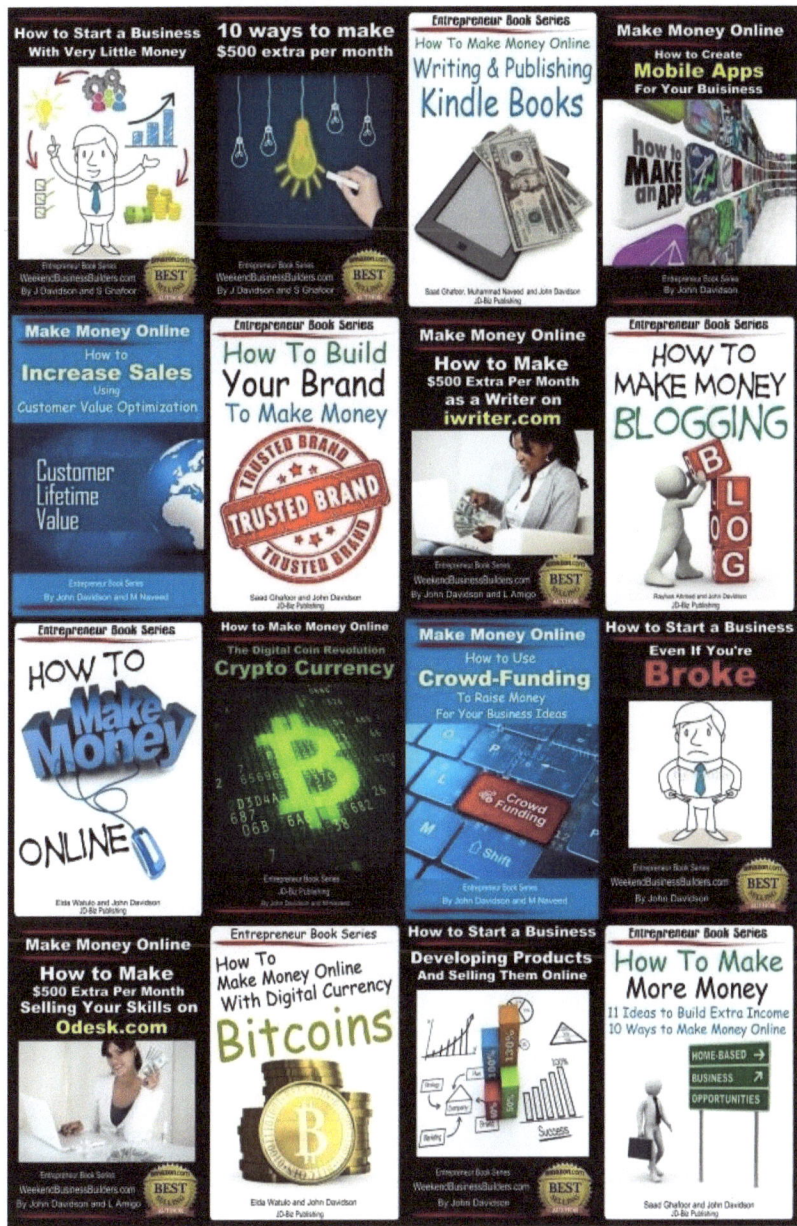

Our books are available at

1. Amazon.com

2. Barnes and Noble

3. Itunes

4. Kobo

5. Smashwords

6. Google Play Books

Download Free Books!

http://MendonCottageBooks.com

Publisher

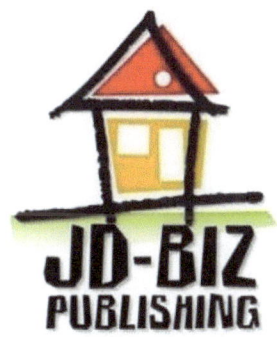

JD-Biz Corp

P O Box 374

Mendon, Utah 84325

http://www.jd-biz.com/

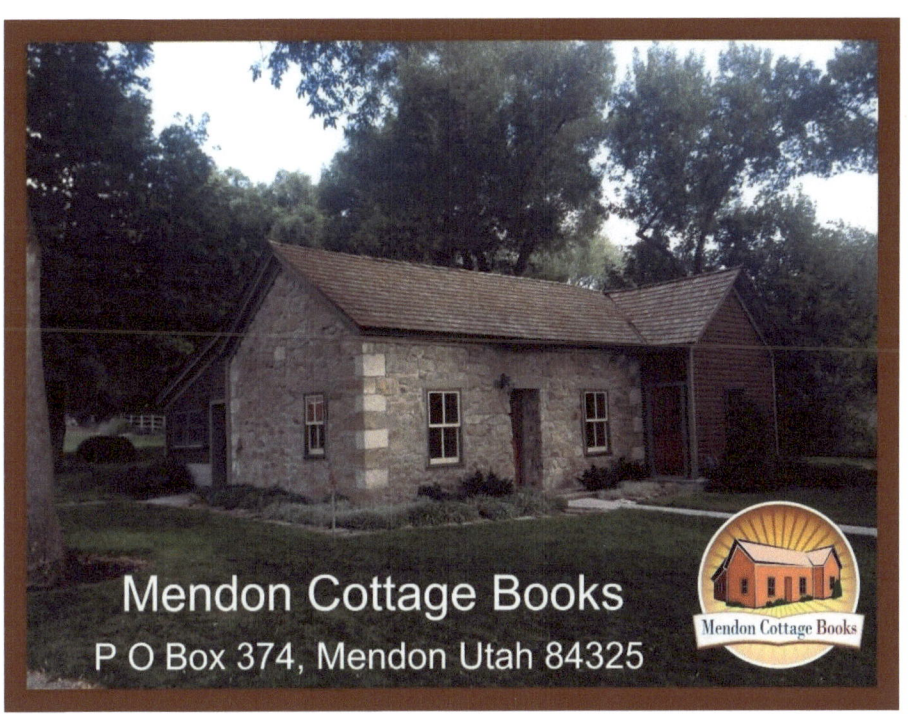

www.ingramcontent.com/pod-product-compliance
Lightning Source LLC
Chambersburg PA
CBHW040918180526
45159CB00002BA/524